C000076882

YOU

ME

summersdale

YOU AND ME

An Hachette UK Company
www.hachette.co.uk

Summersdale Publishers Ltd
Part of Octopus Publishing Group Limited
Carmelite House
50 Victoria Embankment
LONDON
EC4Y 0DZ
UK

www.summersdale.com

Printed and bound in the Czech Republic

ISBN: 978-1-78783-225-1

Substantial discounts on bulk quantities of Summersdale books are available to corporations, professional associations and other organizations. For details contact general enquiries: telephone: +44 (0) 1243 771107 or email: enquiries@summersdale.com.

To..........................

From......................

I love you,
Not only for
what you are,
But for what I
am when I am
with you.

Roy Croft

Love must be
as much a light,
as it is a flame.

Henry David Thoreau

Who, being loved,
is poor?

OSCAR WILDE

In your light
I learn how to
LOVE.

Rumi

SPEAK LOW,
IF YOU SPEAK LOVE.

William Shakespeare

You have made a place in my heart where I thought there was no room for anything else.

Robert Jordan

Love is the enchanted dawn of every heart.

Alphonse de Lamartine

YOU

BRING

OUT

THE

BEST

IN ME

I ask you to pass
through life at
my side – to be
my second self,
and best earthly
companion.

Charlotte Brontë

Do all things with love.

Og Mandino

WE LOVED WITH
A LOVE THAT WAS
MORE THAN LOVE.

Edgar Allan Poe

Love is the emblem of eternity.

Germaine de Staël

I'M ALWAYS HERE FOR YOU

In every living
thing there is the
desire for love.

D. H. Lawrence

We can only
learn to love by
LOVING.

Iris Murdoch

I love thee
with the breath,
smiles, tears,
of all my life.

Elizabeth Barrett Browning

He has achieved
success who
has lived well,
laughed often
and loved much.

Bessie Anderson Stanley

I can live without money, but I cannot live without love.

JUDY GARLAND

YOU MAKE
MY HEART
HAPPY

There is never
a time or place
for true love.
It happens
accidentally,
in a heartbeat,
in a single flashing,
throbbing moment.

Sarah Dessen

She is the heart
that strikes a whole
octave. After her all
songs are possible.

Rainer Maria Rilke

ALL YOU NEED IS LOVE. BUT
A LITTLE CHOCOLATE NOW
AND THEN DOESN'T HURT.

Charles M. Schulz

I love that feeling
of being in love,
the effect of having
butterflies when
you wake up in
the morning.

Jennifer Aniston

They invented
hugs to let
people know
you love them
without saying
anything.

Bil Keane

YOU
MAKE
ME
SMILE

The good life is one inspired by love and guided by knowledge.

Bertrand Russell

In love, one and one are

ONE.

Jean-Paul Sartre

The sound of a kiss
is not so loud as
that of a cannon,
but its echo lasts a
great deal longer.

Oliver Wendell Holmes Sr

I LOVE YOU
TO THE MOON
AND BACK

I have a strong
will to love you
for eternity.

Milan Kundera

Soul meets soul on lovers' lips.

Percy Bysshe Shelley

IN YOU
I HAVE
FOUND
MY
CLOSEST
FRIEND

The madness
of love is
the greatest
of heaven's
blessings.

Plato

TO WITNESS TWO LOVERS IS
A SPECTACLE FOR THE GODS.

Johann Wolfgang von Goethe

Love isn't an emotion or an instinct - it's an art.

MAE WEST

YOU'RE AN ALL-WEATHER FRIEND

There is only
one happiness in life:
to love and be loved.

GEORGE SAND

Love is of all passions the strongest, for it attacks simultaneously the head, the heart and the senses.

Lao Tzu

LIFE IN ABUNDANCE COMES
ONLY THROUGH GREAT LOVE.

Elbert Hubbard

Love is a
game that two
can play and
both win.

Eva Gabor

The best and most
beautiful things...
cannot be seen
or even touched,
but must be felt
with the heart.

Helen Keller

True love stories never have ENDINGS.

Richard Bach

TOGETHER
WE ARE
UNSTOPPABLE!

Where there is love there is life.

Mahatma Gandhi

To love is
to receive a
glimpse of
HEAVEN.

Karen Sunde

WE'RE TWO HALVES OF ONE WHOLE

Romance is the glamour which turns the dust of everyday life into a golden haze.

Elinor Glyn

LOVE WILL DRAW AN
ELEPHANT THROUGH
A KEYHOLE.

Samuel Richardson

Sometimes
the heart sees
what is invisible
to the eye.

H. Jackson Brown Jr

YOU'RE NEVER FAR FROM MY THOUGHTS

Leave a kiss
but in the cup,
And I'll not look
for wine.

Ben Jonson

Love is the greatest
refreshment in life.

PABLO PICASSO

You are my
only love. You have
me completely in
your power.

James Joyce

Love is composed of a single soul inhabiting two bodies.

ARISTOTLE

Too much of a good thing can be wonderful.

Mae West

The Eskimo has fifty-two names for snow because it is important to them; there ought to be as many for love.

Margaret Atwood

Love is a great BEAUTIFIER.

Louisa May Alcott

TAKE
MY
HAND
AND
DON'T
LET GO

I LOVE THEE – I LOVE THEE!
'TIS ALL THAT I CAN SAY;
IT IS MY VISION IN THE NIGHT,
MY DREAMING IN THE DAY.

Thomas Hood

I know of only
one duty, and
that is to love.

Albert Camus

Each time you love,
love as deeply as if
it were forever.

AUDRE LORDE

Those who
love each other
shall become
invincible.

Walt Whitman

Laughter is
the sound
of the soul
DANCING.

Jarod Kintz

YOU MAKE ME LAUGH SO MUCH MY SIDES HURT

Falling in
love could be
achieved in a
single word —
a glance.

Ian McEwan

Anyone can be passionate, but it takes real lovers to be silly.

ROSE FRANKEN

Love is our
response to
our highest
VALUES.

Ayn Rand

Only do what your heart tells you.

Diana, Princess of Wales

Love will
find a way
through paths
where wolves
fear to prey.

Lord Byron

I AM YOURS
AND YOU
ARE MINE

To love and
be loved is
to feel the
sun from
both sides.

David Viscott

Whatever our souls are made of, his and mine are the same.

EMILY BRONTË

When I saw you I fell in love, and you smiled because you knew.

ARRIGO BOITO

We are most
alive when
we are in

LOVE.

John Updike

Everything in our life should be based on love.

Ray Bradbury

YOU GIVE ME
BUTTERFLIES

Being deeply loved
by someone gives
you strength, while
loving someone
deeply gives
you courage.

Lao Tzu

TRUE LOVE BELIEVES
EVERYTHING, AND BEARS
EVERYTHING AND
TRUSTS EVERYTHING.

Charles Dickens

Where there
is great love,
there are
always
miracles.

Willa Cather

I FEEL ON TOP OF THE WORLD WITH YOU!

Love is a
beautiful
DREAM.

William Sharp

A kiss on the beach
when there is a full
moon is the closest
thing to heaven.

H. Jackson Brown Jr

The man
that loves and
laughs must
sure do well.

Alexander Pope

Seize the moments
of happiness, love
and be loved!
That is the only
reality in the world,
all else is folly.

Leo Tolstoy

Let love
steal in
disguised as
FRIENDSHIP.

Ovid

OURS

IS

MY

FAVOURITE

LOVE

STORY

YOU ARE MY HEART, MY LIFE,
MY ONE AND ONLY THOUGHT.

Arthur Conan Doyle

Thus love has
the magic power
to make of a
beggar a king.

Emma Goldman

Love is a canvas furnished by nature and embroidered by imagination.

Voltaire

Kiss me, and you will
see how important I am.

SYLVIA PLATH

I CAN TRUST
YOU WITH
MY DEEPEST
SECRETS

Love makes your
soul crawl out from
its hiding place.

Zora Neale Hurston

Let your love be like the misty rains, coming softly, but flooding the river.

Malagasy proverb

OUR SOULMATE IS
THE ONE WHO MAKES
LIFE COME TO LIFE.

Richard Bach

You should be
kissed and often,
and by someone
who knows how.

Margaret Mitchell

YOU ARE
MY RAY
OF LIGHT

I carry your heart with me (I carry it in my heart).

E. E. Cummings

A heart
that loves
is always
YOUNG.

Greek proverb

**Love
loves to
love love.**

James Joyce

You must allow
me to tell you
how ardently
I admire and
love you.

Jane Austen

Love is not
blind. It is an
extra eye, which
shows us what
is most worthy
of regard.

J. M. Barrie

Life is short. Kiss slowly, laugh insanely, love truly and forgive quickly.

PAULO COELHO

WHAT WOULD I DO WITHOUT YOU?

Love is not
consolation,
it is
LIGHT.

Simone Weil

OUT OF SEVEN BILLION PEOPLE, YOU'RE MY FAVOURITE

When love exists,
nothing else matters.

ISABEL ALLENDE

Love
conquers all.

Virgil

If a thing
loves, it is
INFINITE.

William Blake

KISSES,
EVEN TO THE AIR,
ARE BEAUTIFUL.

Drew Barrymore

Love is being stupid together.

Paul Valéry

If you remember me, then I don't care if everyone else forgets.

Haruki Murakami

What force is more potent than love?

Igor Stravinsky

TWO SOULS ARE SOMETIMES CREATED TOGETHER AND... IN LOVE BEFORE THEY'RE BORN.

F. Scott Fitzgerald

Life is not
measured by
the number of
breaths you take,
but by the moments
that take your
breath away.

Anonymous

The greatest pleasure of life is LOVE.

Euripides

I LOVE YOU MORE THAN THERE ARE STARS IN THE SKY

Love has no age,
no limit; and
no death.

John Galsworthy

You are always new, the
last of your kisses was
ever the sweetest.

JOHN KEATS

Love should be a tree whose roots are deep in the earth, but whose branches extend into heaven.

Bertrand Russell

Nobody has
ever measured,
even poets,
how much the
heart can hold.

Zelda Fitzgerald

I LIKE THAT WE'RE STRANGE IN THE SAME WAYS

LOVE DISCOVERS TRUTHS
ABOUT INDIVIDUALS THAT
OTHERS CANNOT SEE.

Søren Kierkegaard

To love is
so startling it
leaves little time
for anything else.

Emily Dickinson

A kiss is a
lovely trick
designed by
nature to stop
speech when
words become
superfluous.

Ingrid Bergman

Love is
everything it's
cracked up to be...
it really is worth
fighting for, being
brave for, risking
everything for.

Erica Jong

I am in you
and you in me,
mutual in divine love.

WILLIAM BLAKE

MY HEART IS AT HOME WITH YOU

Life is the flower
for which love
is the honey.

Victor Hugo

Love is space
and time measured
by the heart.

MARCEL PROUST

If nothing saves
us from death,
at least love
should save
us from life.

Pablo Neruda

If I had a flower
for every time I
thought of you...
I could walk
through my
garden forever.

Alfred, Lord Tennyson

THEY SAY LOVE IS THE
BEST INVESTMENT; THE
MORE YOU GIVE, THE MORE
YOU GET IN RETURN.

Audrey Hepburn

YOU

BRIGHTEN

UP

MY

DARKEST

DAYS

Love is the magician
that pulls man out
of his own hat.

Ben Hecht

We love
because it is
the only true
ADVENTURE.

Nikki Giovanni

Love is something eternal; the aspect may change, but not the essence.

Vincent van Gogh

No more thou,
and no more I,
We, and only we!

RICHARD MONCKTON MILNES

I think to
love bravely
is the best.

Marilyn Monroe

Love shall be
our token,
Love be yours
and love be mine.

Christina Rossetti

To live is
like to love –
all reason is
against it, and
all healthy
instinct for it.

Samuel Butler

Love is like smiling;
it never fades and
it is contagious.

ANONYMOUS

YOU ARE
MY HAPPY
PLACE

Make me immortal with a KISS.

Christopher Marlowe

Love is like
pi – natural,
irrational, and
very important.

Lisa Hoffman

WHO TRAVELS FOR LOVE
FINDS A THOUSAND MILES
NOT LONGER THAN ONE.

Japanese proverb

Love is the
poetry of the

SENSES.

Honoré de Balzac

My love is
such that rivers
cannot quench.

Anne Bradstreet

One word frees us
of all the weight
and pain of life:
that word is love.

Sophocles

YOU
AND
ME
WERE
MEANT
TO BE

Love is but
the discovery of
ourselves in others,
and the delight in
the recognition.

Alexander Smith

Love is always before you.

André Breton

LOVE
MAKES US
RICHER

**Without love,
the world
itself would
not survive.**

Lope de Vega

The love we give away is the only love we keep.

ELBERT HUBBARD

In love the
paradox occurs
that two beings
become one and
yet remain two.

Erich Fromm

Yours is the
light by which
my spirit's born...
You are my sun,
my moon, and
all my stars.

E. E. Cummings

If you're interested in finding out more
about our books, find us on Facebook
at Summersdale Publishers and follow
us on Twitter at @Summersdale.

www.summersdale.com